DAILY MESSAGES

GOD....HELP THE WAY I FEEL!

GREGORY ALANTAE AND ASHTINE BESTEDA

Copyright © 2024 by Gregory Alantae

Copyright © 2024 by Ashtine Besteda

All rights reserved.

ISBN 978-1-7369929-2-0

EBook ISBN 978-1-7369929-3-7

1.
STUCK

Feeling Stuck? Sometimes you reach a place in life where you feel stuck and there is nowhere to go. I want to let you know that you are not in the wrong place! God has you there for a purpose that you cannot yet see. Sometimes we feel that God has forsook us and forgotten us, when the entire time, He is right there with us! So many times we find ourselves at points where we feel like quitting and giving up. Jeremiah, known as the "weeping prophet," felt quite like you may be feeling. He felt and wished he had never been born because God placed him in *pivotal* position for his purpose![+ Jeremiah 15:10-21] You are not stuck, you are in a pivot.

God is about to re-direct your path. Jeremiah soon reached a point where he could no longer cry about his position. He knew that he simply had to wait on God. When you don't know where to go or which way to turn, just remember: **He is the God of Direction.**

2.
OVERWHELMED

Feeling overwhelmed? Sometimes you reach a place in life where you feel overwhelmed. After trying to hold it together for so long, you reach a breaking point. Elijah is a great reference in relation to this feeling. Elijah was one of the mightiest Prophets in the Bible. In the Text, there is a moment of his life described where he reached a place of utter overwhelmingness. Elijah was so overwhelmed that he asked God to take his life. [1 Kings 19:3-8] You may feel like you have reached your breaking point and that you just can't take anything else, but *God will not let you go out like that!* The Bible tells us that after Elijah was at the height of being overwhelmed (the breaking point), he fell asleep under a tree and God sent an angel to feed him. The angel came to give him the strength he needed for the journey ahead.

    To the one reading this, you cannot quit! God has a greater plan in store for you. I know you feel that you have reached your breaking point, but this is actually your turning point. God has more for you. This feeling that you are experiencing is only temporary. The angel is coming to your place of rest. Get up and be who God has called you to be.

3.
ALONE

Feeling alone? Sometimes you feel like you are all by yourself. I get it! You can be in a room filled with many, but feel like you're the only one in it. God has a way of isolating you for a reason. This period of isolation is where God can truly deal with you how He wants to. You're not alone...**God is with you!** Allow God to deal with you because there is something important that He is trying to show or tell you. He doesn't stop the world for just anyone. When you have this feeling, remember that you are never alone. God wants your attention and He is waiting on you to speak to Him. Ezekiel is a great example of someone who was alone for a period of time. He was placed in a valley of dry bones, dead people. In this valley, he heard a voice in the midst of the dead silence and isolation. A question was asked to Ezekiel: *Can these bones live?* + Ezekiel 37:1-3 Ezekiel knew that he was surrounded by dead people. Dead people cannot speak, silence is the only sound amongst the dead. This voice must be from God. Thus, his response was: *God, only you know!*

Sometimes God has you alone to show you that He is the most important person in your life. You cannot endure this life without Him. Ezekiel could have easily given God his opinion, but instead he Trusted in his God. He trusted that God would bring him through, since God is the one who brought him to the place. God will always make a way for you, but you have to trust that He is with you every step of the way!

4.
REJECTED

Feeling rejected? Like every time you try, you end up rejected and never chosen? It seems like everyone and everything doesn't accept you. I know this is a hard pill to swallow, knowing that you didn't ask for the treatment. Joseph is a great reference for the feeling of rejection. Joseph was given a unique coat of many colors, which prompted him to be rejected by his own brothers. Out of all eleven of his brothers, Joesph was *the one* to receive the birthright. This brewed further rejection from his brothers. So much so that they kidnapped him and threw him into a ditch; they left him to die.

Could it be that the reason you feel this way is a result of receiving something you did not ask to carry? Joseph did not ask for the unique coat; it was given to him. He did not ask for the birthright, yet it was still given to him. There is an anointing on your life that was simply *given* to you. You did not ask for it. You were chosen to receive it. The anointing on your life causes those who do not understand it to reject you. This is for your good.

It is not you that they reject, it is what's *on you*

that makes them upset. Their rejection is between them and God. God makes use of everything and everyone around you to get you to the place that you are supposed to be. Allow the rejection to work for your good.⁺ ^{Romans 8:28} Enlighten your perspective with His Word. When you find yourself feeling rejected, remember: you are *the one*, anointed for what is ahead!

5.
STAGNANT

Feeling stagnant? Like the earth is spinning yet you're in the same spot? Like everything has become so routine and you just can't seem to figure out what to do differently, but you know you need a change? There is a woman by the name of Hannah introduced in the Book of First Samuel, whose story may be of great service to you. Hannah was one of two wives, married to a man named Elkanah. The Scripture tells us that Hannah was barren, unable to receive children, but the other wife was. Every year the entire family would travel to Shiloh to worship and sacrifice to the Lord at the tabernacle. On the days of sacrifice, Elkanah would give portions of the meat to the other wife and her children. Though he loved Hannah, he would only give her one choice portion of meat because the Lord had not given her children. This was the routine: they would go up every year to Shiloh, she would receive her choice portion and be taunted by the other wife for not having children. Scripture states that every year, each time, Hannah would be reduced to tears and would not eat. This was the routine. It was stagnating.

Once, Hannah decided she had enough—enough of the routine grief and tears. She got up and went to pray. She poured her heart out to the Lord, casting all her cares and sorrows unto Him. She made a request to the Lord. The Text states that the priest who found her praying knew not what she requested, but expressed agreement in that God will grant the request she asked of Him. She went back, began to eat and was no longer sad.[+ 1 Samuel 1:1-18]

If you find yourself feeling stagnant in this life, I encourage you to follow Hannah's steps: get up and go pray to the God of Israel. If no one is present to agree with your request in prayer, may this book serve as your agreement in faith that God will grant your request and put an end to your stagnation. He is a God of movement; there is no silence in His presence as the angels worship Him without ceasing.[+ Revelation 5:11-12] He wants to hear from you. May prayer to Him be your first step out of the feeling of stagnation. In Jesus Name, Amen.

6.
LOST

Feeling lost? It seems like you don't know where to go, or who to trust. It seems like you can't find any direction and don't know which way to turn. Sometimes it *seems* like the plan of God for your life leaves you lost and you just can't seem to get on track. Moses felt the same way according to the Bible. Moses felt both, lost and overwhelmed at a point in his life. He ended up wandering into the wilderness for years and did not hear God the entire time. Conceivably, we as God's children can accept the feeling of being lost as a sign that we are on the right track, and most importantly as a reminder that without Him, we have no direction.

It was not until the Israelites cried out to God that Moses received a command to lead them.+ Exodus 2:11-3:22 Perhaps the Lord is preparing your assignment while you're in this season. The Lord spoke directly to Moses, giving him clear directions. God had allowed Moses to wander, and at the appointed time, He gave Moses his orders, steps, and directions. He also promised to be with him the entire time. If God has not told you to move yet, you are not lost...you are in preparation for the assignment

He will soon give you. Await His instructions.

God is the Author and Finisher of our faith.+ Hebrews 12:2 He knows our end from our beginning+ Isaiah 46:9-10, and *He* established the plans for our lives...not us.+ Jeremiah 29:11 He knows where you are even when you do not.+ Psalm 139:1-12 Once you realize He is your guide, the feeling of being lost will subside. Scripture instructs us to trust in the Lord with all of our heart and lean not unto our own understanding.+ Proverbs 3:5-6 Submit to His will and His way for *your* way. Allow the Author's story to flow just as He created it to. **Know that your steps are ordered by the Lord.**+ Psalm 37:23 Continue trusting God in every path that He has you on, even when it gets frustrating and you feel like you're wandering. You do not know the way because you did not create the plan for your life, but **He** knows...and His plan will always be greater than what you can even ask or imagine.+ Ephesians 3:20-21

7.
TIRED

Feeling tired? Like you have had enough, and you are out for the count? It seems like every time you try to stand you get knocked back down. Every time you take one step forward, you get pushed ten steps back and it gets tiring for you. You are not alone. God is releasing strength to you.+ Isaiah 40:28-29

He never promised that the road would be easy, but He did promise that He will never leave you nor forsake you.+ Deuteronomy 31:8 There is so much in store for your life.+ 1 Corinthians 2:9-10 The enemy will try to hold you captive in your mind, and if you do not combat it with the promises and Word of God, the enemy will cause you to become weary. You must remember to meditate on God's Word day and night.+Joshua 1:8 We must not rely on our own strength and wisdom, but solely on the strength and wisdom of the Lord.+ Ephesians 6:10-13 We are consistently reminded through His Word that we are both, welcomed to and encouraged to rely on Him for our help here on this earth (Matthew 11:28-30, Jeremiah 31:25, Psalm 46:1, Psalm 62:1, and Psalm 73:26). Since the enemy is attacking you so heavily, rejoice in the Lord! You are almost there. There is somebody depending on you to finish this course! You got this and God has you!

8.
HEARTBROKEN

Feeling heartbroken? Like every time you put yourself out there, you end up getting your heart broken? You share the love that God gave you and people abuse that love, taking it for granted. Please accept our reminder that He, the Lord God, has the power to heal the brokenhearted.+ Psalm 147:3 I know you may feel broken, like there is nothing else to do because you've given your all and still ended up getting your heart broken.

You have done the right thing by choosing to act in love, but do not get so caught up in the outcome. We are not responsible for the actions and responses of others; we are only responsible for our actions and how we treat others. In loving others, you are obeying the second greatest commandment written in the Law of the Lord.+ Mark 12:28-31 You have done right in choosing to love. The response of the recipient is merely between them and God. If your act of love was seemingly rejected, do not get consumed by the feeling. Instead, go to God and ask Him to keep your heart pure.+ Psalm 51:10 Keep spreading His love. God sees and He knows everything you are going through. He will improve everything concerning you.+ Psalm 138:8 May He begin to heal every wound that you have and cause every broken piece to be mended back together. In Jesus Name, Amen. Remember, He is near to the brokenhearted.+ Psalms 34:18

9.
IGNORED

Feeling ignored? It seems that no one hears you, even when you try to explain yourself. Like everything you say goes out of the window, when you are just trying to help? Perhaps you've prayed and haven't heard God respond; thus, you feel that you've been ignored? Sometimes God is silent because he is working on your behalf. Can you imagine how Sarah felt, hoping for a child throughout most of her adult life? She prayed and God promised to give her a child, yet it just wasn't happening on her time. Sometimes we as humans can mask impatience with the feeling of being ignored.

Consider Jonah as he did everything right while inside the whale, yet he still had to wait on God to have the whale spit him out after three days and three nights.+Jonah 1:17 Sometimes you may not understand it all, but He does. You are not being ignored. God is just working everything out for you. In the meantime, pray to the Lord and ask that He make you whole and ready for the next step ahead. Be still and know that He is God.+Psalms 46:10 There is no God beside Him.+Isaiah 45:5-6 He hears you even when you feel like He has ignored you. I imagine Jonah felt ignored too. Though, you must remember that even when you feel ignored, He is still listening.+ Proverbs 15:29 So do what Jonah did. Keep praying, believing that He always hears you.+ Jonah 2:1-10 Get ready for what He is preparing for you. You will be amazed.

10.
DELAYED

Feeling delayed? Like you are behind and need to play catch up in life. Like you are supposed to be much further in life than where you are right now. Perhaps you have prayed and asked God to do something for you at a set time, but it seems like it has not happened yet. You are feeling this way because sometimes God will delay you to protect you.

Sarah is a great example of experiencing the feeling of being delayed. God promised Sarah a child, and she had to wait 10 years before she could see the promise manifest. Maybe God is not "delaying" you, but rather preparing you. Further, He may be ensuring that when the promise comes, nothing will hinder or destroy it. Ask the Father to prepare you for His promise. Fix your eyes on Him and you will be exactly where you are supposed to be before you know it.

11.
INADEQUATE

Feeling inadequate? Like either God has not really chosen you, or if He did, you do not feel like the right person for the job? Like you are being set up for complete failure? Perhaps you feel like you are not enough and it is hard to believe what God wants you to do. There is a man by the name of Moses in the Bible who has felt the same way you may be feeling. When God called Moses from the burning bush, he felt that he was not enough. God called Moses to lead His people out of Egyptian bondage, but Moses felt inadequate. Moses felt that he was *not* the one called to do the job that God gave him. Yet, he had to realize that he was indeed *the one* called to fulfill the assignment.

No matter your background, experience, or aspirations, God has called you to do a work. He makes no mistakes in His selection for He is perfect. If He picked you, He knew what He was doing when He did it. Sometimes the work God calls us to do may not always make sense. Sometimes we may feel unworthy of the assignment. Please know this: *No matter what your past looks like, God is still calling you to do His work.*

Oftentimes, your "inadequacies" are the very instruments God will use to get His work done through you. Trust and believe that He knows what He is doing and He will get the glory out of this.

12.
GRIEF

Feeling grief? Like a piece of you is missing, a piece that you feel you can't live without. Like there is nothing else to do after the loss. Do you feel stuck at a place in life where you no longer have the strength or joy to continue? Perhaps you've lost someone dear to you and you just can't seem to get the feeling of grief off of you. You want to honor their memory but when you think of them, there is only pain. There is a man named Joshua who encountered grief in chapter one of his self-titled Book in the Bible.

Joshua was Moses' servant; everywhere Moses went, he went. There is a moment in the Text where God speaks to Joshua and informs him that Moses is dead. Can you imagine the feeling Joshua felt when God told him that the one he loved, served, cherished, and followed is now gone? Joshua felt lost, frustrated, and maybe even disappointed. Sometimes God allows events that bring us grief, but through it all, we have to trust Him. Everything God does, He does for a greater purpose. God did not bring you this far just to leave you at the point of grief. When we take our eyes off of the loss Joshua experienced, we see that God had a greater purpose for Joshua. Joshua was to succeed Moses, and he went on to lead the Israelites in conquering Canaan and distribute the land to the twelve tribes of Israel. In other words, Moses' death was the passing of the baton to Joshua. Joshua became a beneficiary of Moses' legacy. Don't get stuck in grief. Always remember that God does not make mistakes. Lift up your heads! +Psalm 24:7 God is in control.

13.
ANGRY

Feeling angry? Like everything keeps falling apart and failing, and it makes you angry? Like God isn't coming through for you quick enough and the result is anger? Perhaps some things aren't moving in the direction you thought they would and now you feel anger drawing near? There is a man by the name of Jonah in the Bible who felt angry, just like you may be feeling right now. Jonah was called by God to prophecy to the city of Nineveh after his encounter with the whale. In the Text, Jonah obeys God and prophesies to the city, not knowing that God would go back on His prophecy. Jonah was sent to warn Nineveh of their coming destruction, so he warned them. As the story continues, the Lord ended up sparing the city of Nineveh, even after forcing Jonah to prophesy its pending destruction.

    Sometimes you will not understand it all. Even after you know that you've obeyed God, <u>but</u> the opposite happens from what He told you. Don't let this lack of understanding produce great anger, and don't let the feeling of anger get the best of you. God still knows best! Even when the outcome does not look like how you expected it to look, trust God!

14.
CONFUSED

Feeling confused? Like nothing in your life right now seems to be working out how God said it would. It feels like you made the sacrifice, but don't see the reward. It leaves you confused not knowing which way to turn or where to go. You know you heard God clearly, but His actions aren't matching your expectations. Remember what Scripture tells us which is that God is not the author of confusion, but of peace.[+ 1 Corinthians 14:33] Don't forget about this one either, which is that the peace of God which surpasses all understanding will guard your heart and mind in Christ Jesus.[+ Philippians 4:7] This means that you may not understand it all, but you must have peace about it all.

God is an all-knowing God, He knows everything, beyond what we can even perceive or attempt to comprehend. Some things will be difficult and/or impossible to understand, and it will leave you confused if you try to understand. Again, you must remember that even though you may not understand what He is doing, His peace still surpasses all understanding. You must keep in mind that His ways are not our ways, and neither His thoughts our thoughts.+ Isaiah 55:8-9 Understand that this feeling of confusion will occur when God is up to something big for your life! Don't let what God is doing behind the scenes make you lose hope that He *is* doing. God knows what He is doing, even when it confuses you. Have peace, knowing that He is working on your behalf right now!

15.
BLINDED

Feeling blinded? Like things are coming at you out of nowhere, blinding you to the point where you can't see what's next for you? Perhaps things are cloudy right now, and you can't see which way you should take or what you should do next? God has a way of allowing you to feel blinded so that He can perform miracles. We often request miracles from God, but many are not willing to endure the blindness His works require of us. He will sometimes position you in the middle of chaos to show you that He is the One who calms the storm.

In the Book of John, Jesus and his disciples see a blind man as they are walking. As we read the story in John chapter 9, we find that this man was blinded not because of his or his parents' sins...the man was blinded because God allowed him to be born blind. God curated every condition and step of his life in blindness to lead him to this moment...the moment where God's power could be displayed in Him.*John 9:1-12 You may be going through a season right now where God is trying to show you His power in your life. Allow God to do what He does best, even when you cannot see what's happening.

Just follow His lead and obey His command. Like the man in this story, you will begin to see and witness His power. Further, your witness to the Power of God will be evidence for those around you to see and hear about His good works. In Jesus Name, Amen.

16.
HOPELESS

Feeling hopeless? Like you just can't see the light at the end of the tunnel? Keep moving forward; there is a reason why you have reached this point. Remember, it is just at the point where your hope ends that God steps in. Consider the prophet, Elijah. Overtaken by fear, he ran away into the wilderness. After a day of hopeless running, he sat under a juniper tree, feeling defeated. He asked the Lord to take his life away; he no longer had hope for the future. Do not be discouraged because Scripture tells us that this was not Elijah's end. Elijah laid and slept under the same juniper tree, and what happened next will instantly restore your hope. As he rested, the Lord sent provision and soon commanded him to keep going.+ 1 Kings 19:1-8

    Don't lose hope! This point of hopelessness is just a resting point to remind you that God is still with you. Sometimes, God will allow these moments to challenge you, and these challenges are designed to both, increase your momentum and re-edify the upward building of your faith. The Restorer is coming, not just with greater hope, but also with everything you need for the journey ahead. Rest. Keep faith that your provision is coming and you will be able to move forward.

17.
TROUBLED

Feeling troubled? Has life thrown you so many punches that you feel you can no longer walk? Consider the woman with the issue of blood. For twelve years, this woman was troubled with constant bleeding and supposedly no cure. Just like you, she had to be reminded of the presence of Jesus and His instant healing power. In the midst of her pain, she had to courage to seek Jesus.+ Luke 8:43-48 She, like most of us, remembered the healing power of Jesus Christ. She remembered that the power of Jesus goes beyond this world and its methods of healing. She knew that if physicians could not fix it, there was only One left who could. That One, we know, is Jesus. Will you boldly reach out for Jesus in the midst of your troubles? His name alone has the power to transform you, to heal you, to bring you peace and an end to your troubles. Jesus saves.

18.
DISAPPOINTED

Feeling disappointed? There is a story about a local fisherman named Simon Peter in the Book of Luke. Fishing was his job. He would go out and fish to provide for his family. One day, he was unsuccessful. I imagine he was disappointed as he washed his nets, preparing to return home empty-handed. There he was, washing his equipment in disappointment...then Jesus stepped in.

Jesus stepped inside Simon Peter's disappointment (boat) and instructed him to go back into the water and cast his net again. Simon Peter decided to release his disappointment and follow Jesus' instructions. After all, what did he have to lose by trying again? With Jesus in his boat for the final try, Simon Peter caught so much fish that the net began to break. *Luke 5:1-11* Will you let Jesus into your disappointment? That is the exact place where He will perform your miracle.

19.
USELESS

Feeling useless? Imagine standing in Naomi's shoes. She had lost her husband and was left with her two sons and two daughters-in-law. She thought that everything would be okay with just her two sons and two daughters-in-law. Suddenly, both of her sons died. Naomi had then lost all purpose. Everything she birthed had died. I imagine she wondered: if I am no longer a wife or a mother, what use am I?

    With no way to provide for herself, Naomi returned to her village and commanded her two daughters-in-law to leave. One daughter respected her wishes and left. The other, Ruth, refused to leave her. Ruth returned to the village with her and promised to never leave her. Seeking ways to provide for their now two-person household, Ruth went out looking for work. She came upon the land owned by Boaz, a relative of Naomi's late husband. Ruth found favor with Boaz and this favor ignited a new purpose for Naomi. Naomi gave Ruth her tips and tools to get Boaz's attention. Next thing you know, Boaz married Ruth and Naomi was taken care of for the rest of her life.* *Ruth 1-4* If you're feeling useless, look around you...who needs your help? Who can benefit from your wisdom and experience? The cure to your uselessness is the person you can help. They may be the link to your purpose and the key to your life-long provision.

20.
NERVOUS

Feeling nervous? Anxious or fearful about what may happen now that the Lord has given you the instructions you may or may not have asked for? May we peruse chapter one of the Book of Jeremiah? In Jeremiah chapter one, the Lord calls Jeremiah. Before we receive the details of the call, the Lord prefaces HIS message with assurance. In my own terms, HE establishes HIS confidence in Jeremiah and his abilities to do the work he is now being called to do...God says that HE knew Jeremiah before HE formed him in his mother's womb. That before Jeremiah was even born, HE set him apart and appointed him to be HIS prophet to the nations. The Lord knew you before HE formed you in your mother's womb. HE set you apart before you even entered into this earth. That's how confident God is that you will complete what HE has created and called you to do. God is confident in you. So, why are you nervous?

Jeremiah responded to God's confidence with nervousness. He was nervous because he felt that he was too young to speak for God. Who are you to tell your creator what you lack? If HE formed you and HE is a perfect God, how can you tell HIM that HE is making a mistake? You may think that you are too old, too weak, too strong, maybe you have a speech impediment, maybe you sweat or shiver in front of crowds, maybe you think you don't have the degree or the skillset, maybe you are feeling just like Jeremiah right now. He felt that he didn't have what he needed to answer God's call. You are wrong. Right after he told God his fear, the Lord told him to watch his mouth. HE told him not to speak his fear of being young because he will go wherever the Lord sends him and he will say whatever the Lord tells him to say. HE told him not to be afraid of people because HE will be with him and HE will protect him. If you believe the Word of God to be true, then this statement is the same for you. Do not be afraid of people. Do not be afraid at all. For God is with you and HE will protect you. You will do and complete what HE has created and called you to do. God is confident in you. Have confidence in HIM. In Jesus Name, Amen.[+ Jeremiah 1]

21.
DESPERATE

Feeling desperate? Like there's no other option available? You've tried everything but nothing seems to be working. You are exactly where God wants you to be. Desperation is the place where Jesus steps in. There was a synagogue leader by the name of Jairus who desperately ran and fell at the feet of Jesus. He begged Jesus to come home with him to save his dying 12-year-old daughter. He didn't know how Jesus would do it, he didn't know if Jesus would agree to do it, he just believed that Jesus could do it. On the way to his home, a messenger came and said that his little girl was dead and there was no use in bothering Jesus now.

Jairus was probably despaired to the point of hyperventilation at this point, but he already had Jesus with him. Jesus encouraged him, telling him to not be afraid and that his faith would heal his daughter. "Just have faith that if you called Me, I'm coming," says the Lord God of all glory. Jesus entered the home of Jarius and everyone was weeping because they believed the girl was dead. Jesus told them to stop weeping because the girl was only asleep, not dead. The crowd laughed at him. People will laugh and mock your faith, but keep holding on to Jesus, keep your faith. Jesus took the little girl by the hand and in a loud voice, He commanded her to get up (so the people who mocked could hear)! At that very moment, the little girl's life returned and she immediately stood up.+ Luke 8:41-56 Your desperation for Jesus will result in a loud miracle. No one will be able to deny the power of God through your desperation. Keep your faith and do not be afraid. When you call Him, He will answer.

22.
UNCOMFORTABLE

Feeling uncomfortable? Like something just ain't sitting right, but you know the Lord is with you? Let's talk about Peter. Now Peter was what I like to call a "privileged child." He was always in Jesus' business, asking questions and coming to His defense. He was committed to being a follower of Jesus. Nothing mattered more when he walked with Jesus. Peter sought Jesus constantly, he went out of his way to get closer to Jesus, to show his devotion. As a result, he sought and asked his way into a deeper relationship with Jesus...BUT what he didn't know was that this deeper relationship required some discomfort. After all, how can you truly trust someone if that trust has never been tested? Peter unknowingly entered into an uncomfortable situation. He and the disciples were deep into the water when they saw Jesus approaching them, walking on the water. They thought it was a ghost, but Jesus confirmed that it was Him. Peter, like always, asked a question and tested the authority of Jesus. To prove to himself that Jesus was not a ghost, he asked Jesus to tell him to come to Him on the water. Jesus told Peter to come."+ Matthew 14:24-33

    Peter sought his way into a one-on-one miracle experience with Jesus. Peter stepped out on faith and began to walk on water. Suddenly, the wind started blowing and Peter became afraid. Holding fear, he started sinking—he started losing his faith because the wind was making his faith-walk uncomfortable. Peter cried out to the Lord to save Him and Jesus reached out His hand and caught him, asking why he doubted. This was Peter's opportunity to reach a new height in trust and relationship with Jesus. Though it was uncomfortable, if he had stayed in that discomfort just a little longer, keeping and increasing his faith, he would have made it all the way to Jesus. Really, if you think about it further, the fact that he was within arm's reach of Jesus lets us know that his faith was really strong. He was basically there, right with Jesus already. He had endured the discomfort and just needed a little extra help in the last part of the miracle. Peter perhaps took his eyes off of Jesus when the wind began to blow...what if he had kept his eyes on Jesus? If you find yourself feeling uncomfortable, you are already walking in the miracle. The fact that you are uncomfortable right now suggests that you are right there, within arm's reach of Jesus. Don't let the discomfort stop you. Keep your eyes on Jesus! Keep your faith. Expect Him to reach his hand out to you. Jesus will fulfill the miracle in your discomfort. The more uncomfortable you get, the closer you get to

Jesus. Keep the faith and bring it up.

23.
UNLOVED

Feeling unloved? Scripture tells us that God is love. To know God is to love. Love and God are synonymous. To feel that you lack love would imply that you lack God. The question now becomes, what led you to feel a lack of God? What led you to feel unloved? Who led you to feel unloved? After you answer that question, you must then consider, was that in God's Will? This may be a difficult question to answer by yourself, and this is why the only Biblical solution we can find is to seek God.+ Romans 12:2

If you feel unloved, seek love. Not in man, but in the One who is love. God. Be very careful not to seek God and His Love in man. In the Book of Samuel, we read about a king named Saul. Saul was anointed by God to be king over Israel, but Saul had a problem keeping himself in God's Will. You may ask, how do I keep myself in the Will of God? You keep yourself in the Will of God when you obey His commands and instructions, when you trust in Him with all your heart, with all your soul, with all your mind, and with all your strength, and when you love your neighbor as yourself.+

[Mark 12:29-31] Saul found himself in a position where many would think that he was no longer loved because the Lord had rejected him, stripped him of his kingship. The Lord rejected Saul because he disobeyed Him. Saul did not follow the instructions of the Lord and his disobedience to God led him to presumably feel unloved.[+1 Samuel 15]

Seek the Lord.[+ Psalm 34:4] This is the cure to your lack of love. For where God is, there is also love. Love comes from God. Seek the Lord your God and you will live in love, abundantly.[+1 John 4:7-21]

24.
UNAPPRECIATED

Feeling unappreciated? Allow me to introduce you to a woman who also felt unappreciated. Meet Martha. One day, on the way to Jerusalem, Jesus and the disciples stopped by Martha's home. Martha was running around the kitchen, distracted by the big dinner she was preparing. Meanwhile, her sister Mary was sitting at Jesus' feet, listening to what He taught. Martha noticed that she was the only one working so she went into the room and asked Jesus, "Lord, doesn't it seem unfair to you that my sister just sits here while I do all the work? Tell her to come and help me." Martha felt unappreciated like her work meant nothing to Jesus, especially since He saw her growing weary, frustrated and overworked while preparing the big dinner.

Here is the interesting part, Jesus did not tell Mary to get up and help Martha cook. Instead, He told Martha that she was worried and upset over details. He added that there is only one thing worth being concerned about. He said that Mary discovered it and it would not be taken away from her.+ Luke 10:38-42 Mary chose to worship God, Martha chose to work for God. Jesus lets us know here that to worship Him is more important than working for Him. You may feel unappreciated because you are not appreciating. When you appreciate God, you won't go looking for appreciation. You won't feel the need for appreciation. Mary knew this. Martha had to learn this. Find your way to the feet of Jesus and worship. You will no longer feel unappreciated because you are now appreciating.

25.
MUTE

Feeling mute? Like you'd normally have something to say, but you're just at a loss for words. This could be good or bad. Maybe you've lost your job unexpectedly or the long-awaited contract just fell through. Maybe you just received some good, unexpected news or, like in the following example, you received some unbelievable news from the One who only speaks truth. Meet Zechariah, the father of Jesus' cousin, John the Baptist. In Luke chapter one, the Lord sends good news to Zechariah through His angel, Gabriel. Gabriel tells Zechariah that his wife, Elizabeth, will give him a son. A handful of verses back, Zechariah and Elizabeth are both described as very old and righteous in God's eyes. Due to his elderliness, this news was quite unbelievable to him, and Zechariah, like many others in the Bible after hearing a Word from the Lord, responded with disbelief. He asked the angel how he can be sure that the birth would happen since he and his wife were so old.

Gabriel, seemingly indignant, re-introduced himself to Zechariah as *Gabriel*, the one who stands in the very presence of God. In my own terms, it seems Gabriel wanted to re-iterate to Zechariah that this isn't a message from just a man who can lie. This is a message from *the angel*, Gabriel. The one who rarely leaves the presence of God. This was a high-level divine encounter and Zechariah's faithless response was like a slap in the face. As we mentioned, God is not a man who lies.[+ Numbers 23:19, Titus 1:2, Hebrews 6:18] When God says He will do something, He will do it. Since Zechariah did not believe Gabriel's message, Gabriel muted him. He told Zechariah that he would be silent and unable to speak until the child was born, and he added that his words would certainly be fulfilled at the proper time. Just as Gabriel said it, Zechariah was muted. He was mute for Elizabeth's entire pregnancy. Once the child was born, they discussed naming the baby Zechariah, but still mute, Zechariah requested a writing tablet and wrote that the baby's name is John. Instantly, Zechariah could speak again. The Word of the Lord was fulfilled.

If you are feeling mute right now, perhaps the Lord is protecting you for your promise. We as humans are often inclined to respond to every event, circumstance, and situation with words. What we say can very much influence our actions and the outcome. Maybe we should consider muteness to be protection. Protection of God's promise. Protection of God's unfailing Word. Protection for us to stay in His Will. Had Zechariah been able to speak during the pregnancy,

He may have aborted the miracle by diminishing the faith of Elizabeth. For Elizabeth's faith was great when she became pregnant. She had no doubts that she would birth the child. In fact, it was Elizabeth's faith and successful pregnancy status that encouraged Mary to believe when the same Gabriel visited her to foretell the birth of Jesus. Your muteness is your protection. Be still, be silent, and watch the Lord perform His miracle at the appointed time.⁺ Luke 1

26.
MISUNDERSTOOD

Feeling misunderstood? Like you're saying everything right but nothing you're saying is being received the way you intend for it to be received? Let's reflect on a man named Jesus. Jesus Christ is the absolute perfect example of a misunderstood man. His entire earthly life, He was misunderstood by family. During His adult life, even His disciples misunderstood both Him and His teachings quite often. The crowds misunderstood and mocked Him. Yet, Jesus kept going. He did not waver in his delivery or His assignment. He knew that every single misunderstood thing He did had to be done in order for God to get the glory. Perhaps the call on your life is supposed to be misunderstood. Perhaps you can look upon this misunderstanding as an indication that you are on the right track, exactly where God needs you to be to fulfill His Will for your life. Press through this feeling of being misunderstood and keep moving forward, like Jesus, so that God can get the glory out of your life.

27.
FAITHLESS

Feeling faithless? Have you lost your confidence in the God of all power? Have you forgotten that He is the very one who put breath in your lungs, made the sun come up, and let you live to see another day? Have you forgotten that: "Many are the plans in a man's heart, but it is the Lord's purpose that prevails"? +Proverbs 19:21-23 Have you forgotten that: "…all things work together for good to those who love God"? +Romans 8:28 Have you forgotten the Word of the Lord saying, "Fear not, for I am with you; Be not dismayed, for I am your God. I will strengthen you, Yes, I will help you, I will uphold you with My righteous right hand.'" +Isaiah 41:10

The Scriptures exist to guide us and consistently remind us that God is always here and He has never failed. Is it possible that you went out on your own and didn't allow God to move in your situation? Is it possible that you made a decision that God did not approve? Could this be the reason why you have lost faith…because the Lord's Will prevailed over your will? Perhaps it is not a matter of faith, but rather a matter of control. Acknowledge that God is the author and finisher of your faith; He is in control. God knows best. He has seen it all; He knows what will happen before it even happens. With that understanding, it is indeed possible and you are encouraged to consider that the Lord is protecting you. Never forget who God is and what He has done for you. This is the remedy to remain faith-full.

28.
IMPRISONED

Feeling imprisoned? Like you've done what you were supposed to do, yet you feel trapped and unable to move forward? Like you don't know where to go or where to turn? The story of Jonah may very well give you exactly what you need to endure this feeling. Thanks to the authors of the Scripture, we may reference the path of Jonah in God's Will. After running from God's instruction, Jonah fled onto a ship and later found himself trapped inside the belly of a whale. While alive in the belly of the whale, Jonah had no choice but to acknowledge the sovereignty of the Lord.[+ Jonah 1-2] While in this completely dark place, with no sense of direction, no way of escape, Jonah was forced to reflect on what led him there.

In his reflection, he realized that he had led himself to this place of imprisonment by running from God. I believe it is quite possible that if Jonah had not been thrown into the belly of the whale, he would have indeed died...the assignment for his life would not have been fulfilled. This imprisonment was essentially an act of rescue for him. The whale protected him from himself. Realizing this, Jonah began to praise and pray to God, repenting for his disobedience and running. It seems that the Lord needed to get his attention and the best way to get it was to throw him inside the belly of a whale to stop him from destroying his life. Now, God's methods are not always the same, yet His principles are. God will do whatever He has to do to get your attention. Consider taking a tool from Jonah's book...praise, pray, and repent. God stepped into the time of life and put you in an inescapable position just to get your attention. The love of The Father may look like punishment here on this earth at times, but if you lean into His presence, you will see and know that all things work together for your good.[Romans 8:28] Seek Him in these moments. You will not be here forever.

29.
IMPATIENT

Feeling impatient? Like the promise feels closer than before, but it should be here by now? Like you have done everything the Lord told you to do, but it still hasn't happened yet? This feeling of impatience is not uncommon to man, but it must be addressed. To be impatient is to attempt to control the fulfillment of the promises of God…it is an attempt to act as God, and this cannot be. We must remember the fact that the Lord will never give us anything that we cannot maintain or keep. If He cannot trust us with it, He will not yield it to us. This is not to say that you will never receive it. This is to enlighten you of the following…if you seek God instead of His promises, you will find yourself ready to receive what He has promised. Before God blesses you with something, He needs to trust that you will not ruin it, that you are prepared for it, and the He can get the absolute glory from it.

    Sometimes there is a delay because you have not proven yourself to be trustworthy. You may ask, how can I prove myself? That very question can only be answered by the time that you spend with God. The time you spend with God will inform you of the process to get to the promise. In Scripture, we find someone impatient by the name of Sarah. She was promised a child, yet it wasn't happening fast enough for her. So, she decided to arrange the creation of a child through her husband and servant...but this was not God's promise. God promised to birth a child through her. Even after this act, birthed from her impatience, she laughed when God re-iterated His promise to birth a child one year from then. [Genesis 18] She disbelieved God; she did not trust that He would fulfill the promise based on her circumstances.

The very reason why you may have become impatient is because your situation, your circumstances do not look suitable for His promise. BUT we must remember that our Father in Heaven is the God of miracles and wonder. He moves to not only confound the believer, but to transform the hearts and minds of the unbelievers. Your promises are not just for you. They are tied to so many destinies. Had not Sarah birthed Isaac from her womb, we would not exist. Though God remained faithful in fulfilling His promise of a son through Sarah, imagine if Sarah waited on the Lord and sought His presence instead of trying to force what only His presence can produce. It is very possible that she would have birthed Isaac much sooner than she did and possibly avoided all the hardship she endured trying to create His promise for herself. I encourage you to keep your faith in God. Remind Him of His promises to you and thank Him in faith, believing that the promise is already here.

30.
OVERLOOKED

Feeling overlooked? Like time is passing...you know that you are gifted, yet it seems that everyone is looking over you? Like maybe you got it wrong and you have not been called by God? I admonish you to ask yourself this question: why am I in a rush? What is driving your desire to be looked upon? God's primary concern about us in this earthly life is the posture of our heart, not the answer to His call. You'll find in Scripture that most servants of God were indeed not concerned or in high expectation of His use when they were called. Take David for example. David had no idea what assignment was waiting for him as he was outside tending to his father's sheep. I imagine he felt that tomorrow would look just like today: tending to the sheep. God had other plans.[+ 1 Samuel 16:1-13]

  Once you take your eyes off of you and place them on the GOD in front of you, your time to be used will happen exactly when it needs to happen. Without the potential fall into pride/sin: assuming that you've been overlooked and not on time. To believe that you have been overlooked is to believe that you know

God's plan for your life. Scripture states, "For I know the plans that I have for you, saith the Lord."[Jeremiah 29:11] Not the plans that He has given to us. God has the plan for your life. You do not. Be careful not to let pride seep into your thoughts about life with God. We exist to worship Him in our everyday lives, on the every-day streets, in the common jobs, and on the stages and screens. No place holds a greater value. The only value that exists is in the Lord God, Jesus Christ. Perhaps this feeling of being overlooked is a signal to get you to look up and acknowledge the One who looks over all. Jesus sees you. You are not overlooked. Trust that God knows exactly what He is doing and that His timing is perfect.[Habakkuk 2:3, Isaiah 60:21-22]

ABOUT THE AUTHORS

Gregory Alantae is the Pastor of Renewed Faith Church in Atlanta, GA, having impacted thousands of lives through his ministry. His pastoral passion is rooted in the love to see souls saved and lives changed for greater. Gregory continues his assignment in teaching and preaching the Word of God to God's people, pleasured with the privilege of being used for God's Glory!

Ashtiné Besteda is the author of *Love Is What Love Does*, a book of poetry. Ashtiné has written and recorded songs, among them "I Believe" and "Connected."

www.ingramcontent.com/pod-product-compliance
Lightning Source LLC
Chambersburg PA
CBHW042321090526
44585CB00024BA/2766